W9-BQS-314

THE LIFE OF
ARTHUR ASHE

Smashing the Color Barrier in Tennis

Series Consultant:
Dr. Russell L. Adams, Chairman
Department of Afro-American Studies, Howard University

David K. Wright

Enslow Publishers, Inc.
40 Industrial Road
Box 398
Berkeley Heights, NJ 07922
USA
http://www.enslow.com

Originally published as *Arthur Ashe: Breaking the Color Barrier in Tennis* in 1996.

Library of Congress Cataloging-in-Publication Data

Wright, David K.
    The life of Arthur Ashe : smashing the color barrier in tennis / David K. Wright.
      pages cm.
    Includes bibliographical references and index.
    ISBN 978-0-7660-6260-3
    1. Ashe, Arthur. 2. Tennis players—United States—Biography. 3. African American tennis
players—Biography. 4. Discrimination in sports—United States. I. Title.
    GV994.A7W76 2015
    796.342092—dc23
    [B]
                         2014027437

Future editions:
Paperback ISBN: 978-0-7660-6261-0
EPUB ISBN: 978-0-7660-6262-7
Single-User PDF ISBN: 978-0-7660-6263-4
Multi-User PDF ISBN: 978-0-7660-6264-1

Printed in the United States of America
102014 Bang Printing, Brainerd, Minn.
10 9 8 7 6 5 4 3 2 1

To Our Readers:
We have done our best to make sure all Internet Addresses in this book were active and appropriate when we went to press. However, the author and the publisher have no control over and assume no liability for the material available on those Internet sites or on other Web sites they may link to. Any comments or suggestions can be sent by e-mail to comments@enslow.com or to the address on the back cover.

Illustration Credits: AP Photo/Marty Lederhandler, p. 4.

Cover Illustration: AP Photo/Marty Lederhandler

CONTENTS

Arthur Ashe poses on the balcony of his New York City apartment on August 21, 1979. He had recently returned from the hospital after suffering a heart attack on July 31.

Chapter 1

PUBLICITY'S GLARE

T he lean man with the wire-rim glasses stepped into the glow of television lights and was immediately recognized as Arthur Ashe. What was happening?— had the first African-American male ever to star at professional tennis decided to face a tough opponent? Was the player who had defeated Jimmy Connors, Rod Laver, and others announcing an end to his retirement? Or was the former Davis Cup tennis captain about to report an interest in some other phase of his favorite sport? And why had Home Box Office (HBO) furnished the sports hero with a large and special room for this news conference?

Sadly, Ashe's appearance in New York City on April 8, 1992, had nothing to do with tennis. Rather, he solemnly told the group of journalists he was infected with the AIDS (acquired immunodeficiency syndrome) virus. He had been infected as a result of a blood transfusion following surgery several years earlier.

The newspeople seemed stunned. They knew of his tennis ability, just as they were aware that Ashe had suffered heart attacks and had undergone two heart-bypass surgeries and a brain operation. But a few may still have assumed that mostly drug users and homosexuals contracted the deadly disease, so they were ill prepared for the former athlete's announcement.

Nor were they ready to see Arthur Ashe display emotion. After all, Ashe was famous for his ability to hide his feelings, whether playing tennis on center court at Wimbledon in England or silently protesting discrimination in front of the White House in Washington, D.C. Today, however, they saw Ashe's eyes fill with tears.

Ashe said he was admitting that he had the disease because a nationwide daily newspaper, *USA Today*, was about to inform its readers of his illness. He said he had hoped to keep the information secret so that his five-year-old daughter would not know he would soon be dead. At the mention of his family, Ashe put his hand to his forehead. The thought of his loving wife, Jeanne, and daughter, Camera, became too much for him to bear. The only sound in the room was the click of cameras, catching one of America's most respected, most disciplined people in a moment he could not control.

Jeanne, standing beside him, took up Arthur's written statement where he left off. The newspaper, she read, "put me in the unenviable position of having to lie [about having AIDS] if I wanted to protect our privacy. No one should have to make that choice. I am sorry that I have been forced to make this revelation now."[1]

Ashe noted that he disliked this invasion of privacy. Since his playing days were over, he felt he should be free to reveal—or not reveal—his disease as he pleased. But the former athlete knew that he was still well known, just as he knew that many medical and other people had helped him keep his secret until now. So he pledged to take up the cause of AIDS. He ended his prepared statement by pointing out that he and his family would have to learn to behave differently. But they would "adjust and go forward," despite the terrible disease and the willingness of some in the news media to point out anyone who suffered from it.[2]

Ashe regained control of his emotions and answered questions for forty-five minutes. No, he said, neither Jeanne nor his daughter, Camera, had tested positive for the AIDS virus. Yes, he felt fine most of the time, and he planned to continue his business career and his social activism. He reminded AIDS patients not to become depressed, since a cure could come at any time. The news conference ended, as did so many events connected with Ashe's life: He left the room even more respected than when he entered.

Always thoughtful, Ashe had spent the previous day writing his statement and phoning family and friends about the news conference. He gave them advance warning to prevent them from being stunned if they turned on a television, tuned in a radio, or picked up a newspaper. Ashe ended up making dozens of calls to tennis stars, attorneys, politicians, and activists, as well as to aunts and uncles. President George Bush learned of Ashe's ailment and personally called to express his concern.

A lifetime of athletics and activism, capped by burning intelligence and a spotless reputation, won for Arthur Ashe one of the highest honors in all of sports a few months later. In December 1992, he was named Sportsman of the Year by *Sports Illustrated* magazine. Ashe, the magazine noted, "epitomizes good works, devotion to family and unwavering grace under pressure."[3] The athlete-turned-businessperson was being honored not for his tennis game, which had once been exciting, but for his character. To understand the character of Arthur Ashe, it is necessary to travel to the Virginia state capital of Richmond and there to examine the past.

Chapter 2

GROWING UP

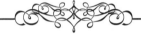

Arthur Ashe, Jr., was one of two children of Arthur Ashe, Sr., and Mattie Cordell Cunningham Ashe. He was born on July 10, 1943, in Richmond, Virginia, the capital of the Confederate States of America during the Civil War (1861–1865). Richmond is a handsome city halfway between the Atlantic Ocean and the Appalachian Mountains. Today it has a population of more than two hundred thousand. Much of the area was burned during the Civil War but recovered quickly because of the tobacco industry. Although it is just over one hundred miles south of Washington, D.C., the Richmond where Arthur Ashe grew up was a very segregated, very southern community.

African Americans in the 1940s were not allowed to sit in the front half of Richmond's public buses. They attended separate schools. There were separate drinking fountains and rest rooms and houses of worship and public parks for blacks and for whites. The races played sports separately, sat in different parts of movie theaters, and ate in different sections of restaurants. Perhaps most important, they had very different views of history.

Longtime white residents of Richmond were proud of their battlefield memorials and their southern heritage. Many black residents knew little or nothing of their own history—their ancestors had been prevented from learning to read or to write, taking the stories of their lives with them to the grave. Yet Arthur Ashe and his family were fortunate. Large, close, and inquisitive, they traced their roots back more than three hundred years to an African woman who survived the frightful voyage from the continent of her birth to Virginia on board an eighty-ton English ship known as *The Doddington*.

A West African as were most slaves, the young woman was known only by a number until she was purchased by a man named Blackwell. She took the name of Blackwell and married a slave with that name. They had a daughter, Lucy, according to Virginia records. She was the first American-born member of Arthur Ashe's family tree. Several generations later, a person on the Blackwell side of the family married a South Carolina native who bore the name of Ashe, from an early governor of North Carolina. The Ashes had a son, Arthur, who married and became the tennis star's father.

How could the Ashe family know this? Fortunately, an aunt still keeps a huge family tree, painted on canvas, with the names of dozens of family members. Each is represented by a single leaf. The tree stands six by seven feet and was put together through years of careful research in old and musty courthouses along the East Coast. In the middle of the tree is a family crest showing a chain with a broken link. The broken chain symbolizes freedom for the slaves. Tennis star Arthur Ashe is the only individual among fifteen hundred family members whose leaf is painted in gleaming gold.

Arthur certainly did not seem destined for stardom on July 10, 1943. He was a small, thin baby, and his lean appearance would stay with him all of his days. He remembered himself as a child with ears that stuck out and legs so skinny that friends and relatives believed he had some sort of disease.

Mattie Ashe, Arthur's mother, died shortly before his seventh birthday. Her death occurred at the pitifully young age of twenty-seven and was caused by a stroke brought on by a problem pregnancy and complicated by a weak heart. She had been ill for some time—Arthur later realized that he often envisioned her in a blue corduroy dressing gown.[1] Arthur, Sr., broke the news of his wife's death tearfully to Arthur and his younger brother, Johnnie, as the three sat on the lower bunk in the boys' bedroom.

"Don't cry, Daddy," Arthur told his father. "As long as we have each other, we'll be all right."[2]

The young boy's words were prophetic. His father kept a close eye on Arthur and Johnnie, and the two boys would do well in school and elsewhere. Young Arthur's father was not educated or wealthy, but one of the jobs he held in the city was an important one—he maintained the parks where African Americans were permitted to play. Part of his job was to keep tennis courts in these parks in good playing condition. Shortly after his mother's death, Arthur stood beside one of the courts one morning watching Ron Charity, Richmond's best African-American tennis player.

Charity was practicing his high, hard serves. He could feel the eyes of the thin, silent boy who lived in the only house in leafy, eighteen-acre Brook Field playground. Charity stopped practicing long enough to approach young Arthur and ask, "Would you like to learn to play?" Arthur said he would. "As casually as that, my life was transformed," Arthur would later remember.[3]

The small, skinny boy quickly learned the rules of tennis. Young Arthur was smart, and tennis is a fairly simple game. The sport is played on a court that is seventy-eight feet long and twenty-seven feet wide. A net crosses the middle of the court and is three feet high. A fuzzy ball is batted back and forth over the net by two or four players (when two people play each other, the game is singles; when there are two each on opposing sides of the net, the game is doubles).

Hitting the ball successfully will send it over the net and into the opponent's court. One player serves, or hits, the ball to the opponent. The opponent tries to return the ball so that the server cannot hit it. Points are scored by the first person who hits the ball inside the opponent's court in such a way that the ball is not returned. A game is won by the first player to score four points.

To make things a bit complex, the first point is fifteen, the second score is thirty, the third point is forty and the fourth is game. If both players have won three points, or have scores of forty, that is a deuce or tie game. To win the game, one player must move two points ahead of the opponent. When a player is one point ahead of the opponent, the score is termed the advantage of that player. If the other player wins the next point, the game returns to deuce, or tie.

A player must win six games to win a set, and he or she must win that set by a margin of two games over the opponent. When the leader is serving and, for example, seven games have been played in the set, the score could be called four-three. When the leader is awaiting the opponent's serve, the score would be announced as three-four. The first player to win two of three sets or three of five sets wins the entire match.

Arthur, Sr., felt his son was too thin for football and other contact sports, and he made him take naps long after other children stayed up all day. He was relieved to see the boy learn the rules of tennis as he swatted madly at the bouncing balls. Young Arthur loved the game and showed real ability. A couple of years later, in 1953, the ten-year-old would pose for a newspaper photo amid a number of trophies. But these were trophies won mostly at Brook Field playground, not at the larger and better equipped whites-only public courts—and certainly not at the whites-only private clubs. Except for an occasional white player who wandered onto his local court, Arthur was unable to compete against most of the good players in Richmond.

Many people, in and outside his family, helped young Arthur with his game. But none did more for him than a former college athlete who took up tennis to stay in shape. Robert Walter Johnson was a rugged man, a baseball player, and a college football player in the days when no helmets were worn. He attended several African-American colleges after World War I, eventually earning a medical degree. Johnson settled into his practice in Lynchburg, Virginia, where he spent some time looking for a sport he could play the rest of his life.

A thoughtful man, Johnson tried basketball and several other sports before picking up a tennis racket. He stuck with tennis because it was not an easy thing for him to master. But master it he did, playing at the local black YMCA and analyzing the games of white players in parks or at private clubs. Johnson thought enough of tennis to enter and win important African-American tournaments and pay for the construction of a court in his backyard.

Johnson decided to organize young African-American tennis players. He wanted to help local boys enter the United States Lawn Tennis Association's national high-school tournament, held nearby each year. The first two boys he entered were overwhelmed by more experienced white players. Was it true what some tennis publications said—that African Americans lacked the subtle touch required to be great players?

Johnson did not believe so. He spent a large sum of money to make his backyard facility an all-weather, enclosed court, and he invited more and more boys to stay at his home each summer learn his favorite game. Living and practicing with Johnson was no picnic: He forced his players to control their emotions on the court. No one was allowed to raise his voice, throw his racket, or otherwise draw attention to himself.

Off the court, he set the children to work raking his yard, maintaining the court, cleaning the dog kennel, making their beds, and more. They were taught which foods were good for them, they learned table manners, and they were told how to act when a lady or an adult entered the room. Johnson's goal, he said, was for the players to be "accepted without being a center of attraction."[4] He knew white people would more readily allow black players on tennis courts if they behaved.

Each year in the early 1950s, boys under Johnson's care would enter the big high-school tournament. Each year they would be beaten, though they were no longer humiliated by their lack of ability. Meanwhile, in 1953,

Ron Charity called Dr. Johnson. A recent college graduate and a ranked player in a national African-American tennis association, Charity told the doctor that he had been teaching a boy for a couple of years who showed promise. Though small, ten-year-old Arthur Ashe seemed to care a great deal about the game, and Charity wanted someone else who was a good judge to see him play.

Chapter 3

A STRONG MENTOR

When Ron Charity and little Arthur Ashe, Jr., walked onto Johnson's court in Lynchburg, the physician almost sent them home. Though Arthur hit the ball well, he looked as if he would fall on his face with each stroke. Johnson had to admit, however, that Ashe was determined. He also realized that Charity had selflessly spent a lot of time teaching Ashe the game.

Charity returned to Richmond, and Ashe batted the tennis ball back and forth across the net. When Johnson or his son criticized a part of Arthur's game, Arthur told them that he played the way Charity had taught him. The physician quickly believed that Ashe was stubbornly unteachable and called Arthur, Sr., to come get his son. The elder Ashe, who knew how to discipline children, drove quickly to Lynchburg and met with Johnson.

Ashe's father was at least as tough in his own way as the doctor. He was authorized to carry a gun and a nightstick while he patrolled Richmond's parks, and when he told groups of kids to change their behavior, he seldom had to tell them twice. After talking with Johnson, he ordered Arthur never again to question his hosts. Then he drove back to Richmond, leaving his son more than one hundred miles away in Lynchburg.

Forever after, Johnson would use the skinny young tennis player from Richmond as an example of an obedient student of the game. Not that Arthur was perfect—another tennis player about his age consistently outplayed Arthur that first summer. The ten-year-olds spent a great deal of time watching the older players, and they were allowed to practice but seldom played organized games or matches. Johnson felt practice now would prepare his players for matches later.

For a young boy, it was quite an experience. Arthur had never seen an African-American family with so much money as the Johnsons. Their house seemed immense, Johnson drove a big, late-model Buick, and there always was money to buy equipment. Not that everything was perfect— Arthur missed his home, and he tired of the hardest chores, which always seemed to go to the youngest players. But each summer, things got better.

Johnson emphasized the backhand shot, since that is the shot most players find difficult. A typical player will "run around" a normal backhand in order to hit the ball in the forehand position. Arthur would have been a great player without a great backhand—he did, after all, have a serve that could be overpowering. But it is safe to say that his slashing backhand is what his opponents feared most and what they still most vividly recall.

Looking back, Arthur said, "Dr. Johnson really guided me from the time I was ten years old until I went away to college. It was under Dr. Johnson that I learned to play tennis."[1] Ashe also gives himself a bit of credit: "If I had been white maybe I wouldn't have had the drive and discipline I have."[2]

Johnson loaded his car trunk with rackets, balls, and bags, then stuffed Arthur and other young players in the passenger compartment and drove the young people to various tennis tournaments. Washington, D.C.; Baltimore, Maryland; Durham, North Carolina; and elsewhere—Ashe and his fellow players saw them all. As Arthur improved, he needed more and better equipment. His father spent at least $1,000 each year on the very best rackets, shoes, and clothing during Arthur's high school days.

As Ashe learned the game of tennis, other things were happening. In 1955, when Arthur was twelve, a black woman in Montgomery, Alabama, refused to give up her seat to a white man on a public bus. The woman was Rosa Parks. She was arrested for her refusal to give up her seat on the bus, and her arrest later resulted in a federal ruling that all Americans should have equal access to public transportation. Combined with a United States Supreme Court decision a year earlier to desegregate public schools, America was undergoing profound change.

Richmond had a line painted on the floor of its buses. Whites could sit ahead of the line, but blacks could not. Arthur recalled climbing aboard a bus one day and plunking down in the seat opposite the driver. Ashe prepared for a great, rolling view of the road but the white bus driver reminded him to move to the rear, behind the painted line. Though the vehicle was virtually empty, Richmond had not yet erased the line separating the races.

Integrated schooling came to Richmond more peacefully than elsewhere. In Alabama, Arkansas, and Mississippi, white residents protested, hazing African-American youngsters as they were escorted into school buildings by federal troops. Perhaps because Virginia is farther north, the change took place with fewer incidents. On the other hand, a number of white parents enrolled their children in private schools, which were free to admit or deny any child. One of the standards such schools chose, of course, was race.

Many white Americans outside the South had little or no idea of the way in which black residents were treated. However, once television coverage showed African Americans being beaten, jailed, and even killed for civil rights, public opinion moved firmly behind full integration. Yet there was a contradiction—northern cities became segregated as white people moved out of neighborhoods they considered too black. And in the area of jobs, African Americans still suffered discrimination everywhere.

Arthur and his father followed the events of the late 1950s each evening in the newspaper and on television. While adults were laying their lives on the line for equal access to schools and more, young Arthur studied and worked on his tennis game. His father never permitted him to stay out late, much less join a protest. Later, he would think about integration and admire the black and white Americans whose sacrifices made the country more nearly equal. Several would become close friends.

The young tennis players and other African Americans were reminded constantly of racism in the 1950s. Johnson attempted to enter Ashe in an important junior tournament when he was fifteen, but the organizers refused to process the application. A year later, an application for tournament play was received too late, white officials claimed.

Since Arthur was so much better than the local competition, Johnson wanted him to play against better players, who usually were white boys from up and down the Atlantic Coast. Failing that, the physician entered Ashe in the American Tennis Association (ATA) tournaments. The ATA was a separate tennis body primarily for black adults. Arthur won the ATA junior tournament at the age of seventeen. Then he won the men's singles championship that same year. Clearly, he was competitive against anyone.

Arthur was intelligent, earning good grades in school. "He was never a playful child," an uncle remembers. "Even as a young boy he was very private."[3] He was lucky—his father had less patience with Arthur's younger brother, Johnnie, who was a livelier child. African Americans who showed Arthur's kind of progress could count on being attorneys, doctors, or some other professional member of the African-American community. But the boy spent his spare time playing tennis. By the time he was in high school, he had reached a point where there was no one around he could not beat. When Arthur got the opportunity to attend his senior year of high school in St. Louis in connection with a tennis program, he quickly accepted.

"That was where my game really developed," he wrote later.[4] In Virginia, Arthur's tennis game had been somewhat timid—he stayed in the back of the court and simply returned shots, awaiting an error by his opponent. But in St. Louis, Ashe's maturing body added speed to his serves and accuracy to his returns. Equally important, he worked hard in school, graduating at the top of his class.

The final year of high school was somewhat similar to Richmond in that Arthur attended an all-black school. He competed successfully against more and better tennis players of all races in St. Louis, though he missed being with his father and brother. Arthur was seen as a goody-goody by friends, especially those who did not know how strong an influence Ashe's father played in his life. An incident shortly before his eighteenth birthday pointed this out.

Arthur was the only African American in the Middle Atlantic Junior Tennis Championship, held that year in Wheeling, West Virginia. One night during the contest, several white teenaged players trashed one of the cabins where others in the tournament were staying. They blamed the vandalism on Arthur, who had nothing to do with it.

Arthur called his father when he reached Washington, D.C., to tell him of the incident. His father asked Ashe only one question: "Were you mixed up in that mess?"

"No, Daddy, I wasn't," young Arthur said.[5] The elder Ashe never mentioned the matter again, realizing that his son would not tell him a lie.

Arthur's father was as remarkable, in his own way, as young Arthur. The elder Ashe supported his family with a number of jobs besides taking care of the park. He worked as a landscaper, a gardener, a contractor, a builder—whatever it took to feed, clothe, and house his two children. Before Arthur was grown, he helped his father build a new house in Gum Spring, outside of Richmond. Much of the material for the ranch-style home was recycled refuse from a nearby highway project.

Until his father's death in 1989, Arthur worried that misbehaving anywhere on Earth would result in his father finding him and giving him a beating. Even when Arthur was a father himself and could laugh about pleasing his own father, making Arthur Senior proud was always terribly important.[6]

Ashe was accepted in 1961 at the United States Lawn Tennis Association's Interscholastic Championship. The only African American entered, the teenager won without losing a set. Arthur recalled his feelings after realizing that he was the best high school tennis player—regardless of color—in the United States. "It was conceivable that I might win someday at Forest Hills," where America's top adult tournament was held each year.[7]

Chapter 4

COLLEGE AND BIGTIME TENNIS

Meanwhile, the lanky young man was growing and maturing. And he was learning. During his final year of high school, he decided to attend the University of California at Los Angeles (UCLA). He was given a scholarship there, though not strictly for his tennis ability. Arthur was an excellent student, capable of competing with anyone in the classroom, much as he could compete with anyone on the court.

Ashe was not the only tennis player recruited by UCLA. Also headed to the West Coast was Charlie Pasarell, a Puerto Rican whose game was very different from Ashe's. Pasarell did not have Arthur's lightning speed, yet no one ever hit the ball better than did this handsome son of a wealthy island businessperson. Ashe and Pasarell, two outsiders, became close friends and roommates and would remain friends for years.

At first, Ashe wanted to become an architect. His high-school grades in Richmond and St. Louis were almost all As, and he could have chosen any kind of career. However, his college tennis coach talked him out of studying architecture. If Ashe was as good at tennis as he appeared to be, he would need to know how to invest his winnings. Majoring in business would teach him to invest—and it would provide more time to play tennis while in school.

California had a more tolerant view of race, yet barriers remained. Ashe was not allowed to play as a guest at an exclusive club. Interracial dating was accepted by students, but not by everyone else. One young woman's mother did not learn that Ashe was African American until she saw him on television. The daughter had not mentioned the color of her boyfriend's skin in telling her mother about him.

Ashe's college career involved more tennis and study than socializing. He had always been well spoken and a thoughtful writer, and UCLA improved his skills. There was no need to worry about speaking ability or manner. Johnson had seen to it that Ashe and all the other young African-American tennis players who gathered in Lynchburg each summer knew how—and when—to talk.

Four years after proving he was the best high-school player in the country, Arthur proved that he was the best in college: In 1965 he won the United States Intercollegiate singles championship. That same year he graduated with a bachelor's degree. What lay ahead for him now that his formal education was over?

Arthur Ashe, Jr., was not the first African American to play big-league tennis. Althea Gibson, a tall and graceful woman born in South Carolina, became the first African American to play at Forest Hills, New York. She did so in 1950, winning the United States women's singles there in 1957. Gibson's debut was preceded by one other person: Reginald Weir, a New York City physician. He was permitted by the United States Tennis Association to play in an indoor event in 1948. Like Ashe, Gibson was spotted early by the same Dr. Johnson who coached Ashe and a number of others who became good African-American tennis players.

If the white, upper-class heritage of tennis was occasionally wearing on Ashe, it was constantly very trying for Gibson. Those who knew her away from the game found her a warm and friendly person. Once she got near a tennis court, however, she became suspicious of the motives of people around her. Would some treat her kindly, only to turn on her? Were those who rooted for or against her doing so because of race? Had there been no segregation, the woman who grew up in Harlem probably would have won even more than her eleven major tournament titles. But she was not permitted to play in an important tourney until the age of twenty-five.

Exiting college in 1965, Ashe was an amateur, a nationally ranked player, and a recognized name. Most of the major tournaments were for amateurs, which left the pros with little to do except move from city to city, putting on exhibitions before crowds that varied in size.

In 1963 Ashe was selected as a member of the amateur Davis Cup team. As such, Ashe played internationally before he had even graduated from UCLA. After college, he found out about the move toward open tennis. Before the 1960s, amateurs and professionals did not play each other. That changed in 1961 when Jack Kramer, a legendary player a few years earlier, signed many of the top amateurs to professional contracts. Kramer did this because he and many others wanted open tournaments—competition in which either amateurs or professionals could play. But the people who ran tennis tournaments opposed the open-tennis concept.

More and more of the best players, from Australia's Rod Laver to America's Richard (Pancho) Gonzales, signed on to play professionally in 1967. Within a few short months, the best amateurs were all professionals. "If anyone was ever going to see them again at Wimbledon and Forest Hills," said a tennis fan, "the (governing body of tennis) had to make an accommodation. Open tennis came about so fast after that, it was pitiful."[1]

Ashe was momentarily distracted by other events. He was drafted in 1967 into the United States Army. The military made him an officer, gave him a place to live at the United States Military Academy in West Point, New York, and allowed him to play as much tennis as he chose. His service, from 1967 to 1969, came during the Vietnam War. As a celebrity, he did not have to face combat.

Meanwhile, Ashe quickly learned of the difference between amateur and professional players. He beat Dutch professional Tom Okker in the finals in 1968 to take the United States singles championship. But because Arthur was an amateur, he received $28 per day for expenses, while Okker took home $14,000! Ashe was a bachelor living in modest military quarters. He was teaching cadets data processing, and while the Army generously allowed him to play in the major tournaments, he was not getting rich. But several pros were living lavishly and raking in the money.

Before 1968, some of the top amateurs had insisted on being paid secretly to play in tournaments. They would play for fame in the very best tourneys, but promoters who wanted more attention for their matches had to sneak money to the well-known amateur participants so that they would show up. Life got easier with the advent of open tennis, but not all players were able to take advantage of it. Teams from Eastern Europe frequently were forced to turn over any prize money to their governments.

Changes also took place in Europe, where many tournaments are played, in 1968. Many players and those who followed the sport agitated for change, and change came about in England. The British late in 1967 proposed a limited number of open tournaments each year, but those who governed tennis decided against the proposal. British tennis had an ace up its sleeve, however—Wimbledon, near

London, was the site of the world's most prestigious tournament. English tennis people voted overwhelmingly to run all of their tournaments openly and that move broke the back of amateur-only competition.

Or did it? the International Tennis Federation quickly created these four classes of tennis players:

- Amateurs who would not accept prize money.
- Teaching professionals who could compete with amateurs only in open events.
- "Contract players," who negotiated independent deals to play in tournaments and apparently were true professionals.
- "Registered players," who could accept prize money in open tournaments but who kept their standing for the Davis Cup and other amateur events.

This was not an ideal situation for the pros, since their reputations were on the line. How would it look if several pros entered an open tournament and were beaten by a bunch of amateurs? In turn, the amateurs feared the awesome reputations of the more experienced professionals. As it turned out, Ashe had little to fear.

A pioneer in many ways, Arthur Ashe stunned the tennis world by winning the first U.S. Open in 1968 as an amateur player. Fans also noted that it was the first win by an American of the big annual tournament at Forest Hills, New York, since 1955. During a time of enormous civil strife, and with African-American athletes protesting the Olympics in

Mexico City, Ashe's victory was savored by tennis fans and nonfans alike. No wonder he ended the year ranked as the number one tennis player in the world.

Open tennis lured money—big money—to the game. Networks and sponsors scrambled to put tennis on TV in America and many other nations. Many tournaments with famous sponsors were played and then broadcast months later, once a network had edited the footage, found the sponsor, and sold advertising time. The big beneficiaries were the players. Rod Laver, the wonderful left-handed player from Australia, earned more than $200,000 in 1979 from prize money alone. He, Arthur Ashe, and dozens more became truly world famous. They enjoyed lucrative deals to endorse clothing, shoes, rackets, and other sports and consumer products.

Ashe was by 1970 not only a professional tennis player but a well-to-do professional. He had served his hitch in the military, and life was as exciting as it might ever get. In *Arthur Ashe—Portrait in Motion*, a book he co-wrote with sportswriter Frank Deford, Ashe tallied his travels in a typical year. He made 129 airplane trips, slept in 71 different beds, and logged 165,000 miles.[2] Entries in the diary-like book were made in such far-flung places as Tokyo and London, Cape Town and Los Angeles, Madrid and Tucson, Sao Paolo and Montreal, Denver and Paris, and Hilton Head and Nairobi. Ashe seemed almost out of place whenever he unlocked the door to his own apartment in New York City.

Ashe had much on his mind. He and fellow tennis-playing globetrotters were trying to form their own association, one that would ensure fair treatment of players by those who administered the game, as well as by television networks, sponsors, agents, and manufacturers. The Association of Tennis Professionals, or ATP, came together in 1972. Immediately, these united male touring pros made playing and tournament conditions more nearly uniform. A total of fifty players paid $4,000 each to join, naming retired tennis great Jack Kramer as their executive director.

Ashe, as in everything, became deeply involved in the worldwide affairs of the ATP. His flights from one tournament to the next were not relaxing stretches where he could read a good book but were instead filled with memo-writing, calculating, and dictating into a small tape recorder. None of the players were prepared for the public acceptance of tennis, a boom that had the folks next door getting up early on weekend mornings to get a public court, then spending part of the afternoon watching a televised tournament. With his sparkling reputation, Ashe served as president of the Association of Tennis Professionals for two years.

Ashe's tenure as president followed the biggest test for the young organization. In 1973, a young Yugoslav player named Nikki Pilic was barred by tennis officials from playing in the annual tournament in Wimbledon, England, because he had decided not to represent his country in Davis Cup tournament play. Pilic was a member of the ATP, and he turned to Ashe and others for help. The association warned that it would boycott Wimbledon if the ban remained. Officials refused to let Pilic play, and the English tournament was a hollow husk of its usual glamorous and talented self. Out of this confrontation, the ATP grew even stronger.

Tennis players have not always been in command of their fate. The game, invented in France and played in earnest in the United States from about 1900, was for many years an amateur sport. Part of the reason for this emphasis on the amateur was that the game was favored by America's wealthiest people—and they did not need prize money. There were few public courts in the 1910s and 1920s, so those who became accomplished players did so mostly at exclusive private clubs. Bill Tilden, America's best player throughout the 1920s, did better playing for expenses as an amateur than in playing for prize money as a pro beginning in 1930. With the Great Depression of the 1930s, not many young people would be exposed to tennis.

Several Californians who were excellent athletes brought tennis into the spotlight just before and immediately after World War II (1939–1945). Don Budge, Jack Kramer, and Alice Marble were capable of beating the world's great players, which they did rather frequently. Good players became pros and later produced good players while serving as instructors. Those who did well with their rackets in the 1950s included Maureen Connolly, Althea Gibson, Dick Savitt, Frank Sedgman, Vic Seixas, Billy Talbert, and Tony Trabert. Among the men, however, no one was more successful than a string of stunning Australian players.

The Australians were neither rich nor pretentious. Instead, they were extremely well conditioned, and they practically owned the Davis Cup and other major tournaments. Names such as Mal Anderson, Ashley Cooper, Lew Hoad, Merv Rose, and Ken Rosewall were only occasionally beaten by stars such as America's Richard Gonzales and Peru's Alex Olmedo. Tennis courts sprouted in city parks all across the country, even in the black recreational confines of Arthur Ashe's boyhood Richmond. All you needed was a racket, a couple of balls, a pair of tennis shoes, and the ability to withstand the heat of a shimmering summer day. Little by little, tennis was becoming a sport for all Americans.

Arthur Ashe made enough money as a professional from 1969 to 1979 that he could coast afterward. Part of his financial success was Ashe's ability to pick good advisors. Yet purses at the start of his career were puny compared to today's huge rewards for championship play. When Arthur won the first U.S. Open in 1968, the total payout was $100,000, with $14,000 to the winner (if he was a professional). In contrast, the purse in 1992 was more than $8.5 million, with the winner in men's and women's singles receiving $500,000 each.[3]

Like so many sports, tennis has become big business. That is the price the sport had to pay to treat participants equally, and Arthur Ashe helped ensure that all players would be adequately rewarded.

Chapter 5

COMPETING FOR THE DAVIS CUP

Emotion seldom overcame Arthur Ashe in public, but his steely calm once failed him at a dinner in Portland, Oregon.

Always an interesting speaker, Ashe was called upon to make some remarks on the eve of a Davis Cup semifinal tennis match between the United States and Australia. The two teams had admired and respected each other down through the years, becoming friends despite the intense rivalry. Ashe began to talk about the quality and quantity of friendship he had experienced in Australia with that country's players. Gradually, he choked up, unable to speak.

Harry Hopman, the elderly Australian who had captained many great teams, got to his feet and told humorous stories to give Ashe time to recover. Ashe began to talk again but could squeeze out only a few more words before once again losing control of his emotions. Described in the press as icy and reserved, Ashe's feelings proved two things at the dinner: Ashe was, beneath his cool exterior, a man who loved and valued friendship. And Davis Cup play was an incredible experience.[1]

Ashe admitted in an article he wrote for *World Tennis* that both the high and low points of his career involved Davis Cup action. The high point, he said, was helping to regain the cup for his country in 1968 from Australia, despite losing a match to Australian Bill Bowrey. The low point took place in 1967 when he lost two singles matches to unranked and unknown Ecuadorans in Davis Cup play. In all, Ashe played thirty-two Davis Cup matches, winning twenty-seven.

What was this Davis Cup, anyway? The huge silver bowl was donated by Dwight Filley Davis, a Harvard University student, in 1900 to encourage international tennis competition. Originally, only the best team from the United States and the best team from Great Britain contested the trophy. Teams from Australia, Canada, and Germany entered the contest a few years later. A record sixty-two nations played in Davis Cup competition in 1984.

The point of the big punch bowl has not changed. Each year, the competition answers one question: Which nation has the world's best team of tennis players? Down through the years, the answer has changed frequently. Most often, American, Australian, British, and French players have captured the cup. But so have teams from Czechoslovakia, Italy, South Africa, and Sweden.

Not all the tough matches were for the cup, of course. One, against fellow American Clark Graebner, became the subject of a book, *Levels of the Game*, by John McPhee. The only book devoted entirely to a single tennis match is *Levels of the Game*. The fact that Arthur Ashe stars in the book says much about his tennis ability.

The match was played at Forest Hills in 1968. It was a semifinal in the United States Open Championship, in which both amateurs and professionals competed for the first time. Amateurs and pros had never before been mixed, and amateur Arthur Ashe was regarded in the tournament as only the fifth-best player present. Several foreign players were favored to meet in the finals.

But here was Ashe, one of four men still alive in the tourney. The winner of the match between Ashe and Graebner, both Americans, would face either an Australian or a Dutch player in the finals. *Levels of the Game* tells how virtually every point was scored between the two Americans. But it tells much more.

The book reports what went through the players' minds, how they got to this level of play, who they are, who influenced them, and what kind of people they were. Ashe and Graebner, black and white, could not have been more different. Ashe's background was modest, though he and Graebner were both college graduates. Ashe grew up at the low end of the middle class, while Graebner was the son of a well-to-do suburban Cleveland couple who catered to their son's athletic urges.

Both players were determined, but very different in terms of temperament. Arthur was calm on the outside, whereas Graebner constantly criticized himself during play. The two were good sports, and they liked and respected each other. But their games could not have been more different.

Graebner played a powerful game that centered around hitting shots he knew would go into his opponents' court. He waited conservatively for whomever he played to make a mistake or to be overwhelmed by his lightning-like serve. Even when he had the opportunity, he seldom hit chancy shots. His forehands were powerful.

Ashe played an unpredictable game based on hitting chancy shots that were dazzling to watch—if they did not hit the net or fly wildly out of bounds. Ashe also had a rocketing serve, but his best shot was his backhand. Few players favor backhand hitting, but Ashe was one of them. He constantly went for improbable shots, even when a game or a set or even a match was on the line. In contrast to his flashy on-court game, the young African American appeared icy calm.

But Ashe was not always as composed as he seemed. In another book, he said:

I never *look* like I'm choking. I'm a slasher, a free swinger, so I always appear loose—but that can be very misleading. Like right now, when I'm nervous on the court, I have an actual difficulty in breathing. And that problem is compounded when I try to run. My legs move stiffly, and soon my whole body offers only the most deliberate movements. It's as if I've lost all instincts for playing tennis, so that my mind must try to explain repeatedly to my body what it already knows how to do.[2]

Both players were born in 1943. Both wore glasses. As children, the two were very much unlike. Ashe never veered from tennis once he began to play. Graebner—larger, heavier, and stronger—played baseball and was an exciting ice skater. His parents would not permit him to play hockey, and they told him he should decide which he wanted to play, baseball or tennis. Graebner put away his bat and glove and concentrated on tennis. The two first met at the age of twelve or thirteen, in a barely remembered tennis tournament.

There were other differences when the two played in 1968. Graebner was married; Ashe was single. Clark and his wife lived in New York City in a high-rise apartment on fashionable East Eighty-sixth Street. Arthur, a United States Army lieutenant, lived modestly at the United States Military Academy in West Point, New York. The Graebner apartment was so neat it looked like it could be featured in a magazine.

Ashe, who disliked order, lived amid a clutter of books, unopened mail, and a closet light that burned nonstop for fourteen months because no one turned it off![3]

Ironically, each of the players had quite a bit to live down. Ashe, of course, still caused suspicion among some white people. What was he trying to prove? they asked each other. Did he want to play big-time tennis, or was he merely part of the new wave of activism that was sweeping the country in the 1960s? As for Graebner, an earlier back injury caused him to walk as if he were strutting. Fans felt he was cocky. Luckily for both men, such meaningless drivel disappeared when either tossed a tennis ball high in the air from the baseline and sent a searing line drive into the opponent's court. Both were quite serious.

Levels of the Game goes inside each player's head in crucial moments during the match. Here a big difference surfaces—Graebner is all tennis, whereas Ashe's mind wanders. Ashe admitted that he had trouble concentrating, no matter how intense his opponent or how important the game. Most often, he thought of food, which was really strange in view of his long and lean appearance.[4]

In contrast to many of today's players, both were extremely polite. Ashe had been told early in his career that he would get four or five bad calls by officials during each match and that he should accept them. Graebner looked to his wife in the stands after each point. He either felt he was about to overwhelm whomever he was playing or he cursed his luck. Both of the twenty-five-year-olds were at the peak of their playing careers.

Being sportsmanlike did not always mean that a match would go smoothly. For Graebner, he would go on to play a National Indoor match in 1973 in Maryland against one of the most boisterous and naughty players ever, Romania's Ilie Nastase. Clark complained quietly, and Nastase shrieked about the nearby click-click-click of a typewriter being used by a *Washington Post* reporter who had to get his tennis story to the morning daily newspaper on time. Fans shushed the reporter, who continued to type. The writer's stubbornness resulted in a fan scratching him, grabbing the offending typewriter, and running off with it! How could a player concentrate with that kind of sideshow?

Ashe, the milder of the two, would play a part in an even stranger story involving Nastase. Ashe had seen or personally experienced the Romanian's abusive tactics for several years. Once, during an important tournament, Nastase called Ashe an unspeakable name. He constantly stalled and teased, baiting whoever was unlucky enough to draw him as an opponent. At the Masters Tournament in Sweden in 1975, Nastase taunted Ashe, and Ashe walked off the court, refusing to play further amid the bad behavior and the insults. Ashe was awarded the match—but Nastase went on to win the tournament because it was a double-elimination contest.

Besides being teased, straight arrows like Ashe and Graebner were sometimes cheated out of games, sets, and matches. Robert Johnson had taught his young African-American tennis players to go after any ball that was two inches or less outside the line, since he assumed that white officials would favor white players. During Davis Cup play in Romania in 1972, officials made so many bad calls that even the Romanian players knew what was going on. One of the Romanian stars actually led the crowd in taunting American players while officials called faults (rules infractions) against American players who were hitting serves the Romanians could not return.

With that kind of activity, Ashe and Graebner probably looked forward to playing each other, no matter the circumstances. There was no funny stuff, just intense action. Ashe's most obvious mannerism was silently pushing his glasses up the bridge of his nose with one finger after a big point, win or lose.

Gradually, Ashe gained an edge in their match. His loose, slashing game—on this day, anyway—was better than the conservative game of Graebner. But Ashe was not always a player who took chances. Charlie Pasarell remembered playing Ashe and thinking that opposing the collegiate Ashe was like hitting balls against a backboard. Ashe returned everything, and returned it well, but there was no emotion in his game. That changed after college. Pasarell noted:

He's alive now. He is more concerned about things—about racial problems, family, business, his friends, his game. He is a little more careful now of what he does. He's more involved in the match, more emotionally involved, and that is why he has become a great, great tennis player.[5]

Ashe did not just get better. As the afternoon wore on, he became unbeatable. By the fourth set, "his game is so big now that it is beyond containment," McPhee writes. Graebner hits blistering serves and returns, and Ashe sizzles them back past Graebner even faster than the muscular Ohioan has sent them to him. Graebner is as impressed as the crowd.[6] The two reach match point—if Ashe wins the next point, he wins the entire match. Graebner hits his first serve into the net. The second serve is hit to Ashe's backhand, and, once again, Ashe smokes the ball into Graebner's court and past him.

Ashe went on a few days later to beat Holland's Tom Okker, winning his first U.S. Open. That match, with the very fast amateur beating a professional so quick on his feet the press called him "The Flying Dutchman," made sports pages all over the world.[7] But it was no better than the Ashe-Graebner contest a few days earlier. Ashe played so many matches in so many countries that the tournaments and the players became a virtual blur. But the level of his game was such in 1968 that he would become the world's top-ranked player at the end of the year.

Chapter 6

CONFRONTING APARTHEID

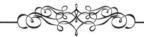

"No word from South Africa," Arthur Ashe wrote in his diary in the fall of 1973. "If the cabinet met last night, they either tabled me or aren't prepared to let me know their answer yet."[1]

Though Ashe was in Madrid, Spain, suffering from jet lag and from being buffeted on the court by the cool weather, his mind was on an appointment he sought below the equator. South Africa was a hotbed of tennis enthusiasm, but it had been shunned by many nations for separating the races and treating nonwhites terribly. Because of Ashe's race, he seemed to be fascinated with the country, which lies at the southern tip of the African continent and was then run by a minority population of Dutch and English descent.

Separation of races began in earnest a few years after World War II in the large, beautiful, and abundant land. Called apartheid, this racial policy severely restricted black Africans to low-paying jobs. They were not permitted to run for office or vote, and they could only live in areas designated all-black. Others felt the same sting of prejudice—persons of East Indian or others of nonwhite heritage did not have the same rights as white Africans, though they were much better off than the Bantus and other black tribes. Black leaders such as Nelson Mandela were imprisoned for political activity that would have been legal in most other countries.

Ashe was notified of his acceptance for tournament play in the country on Halloween 1973. A few days later, he learned that the International Lawn Tennis Federation (ILTF) simultaneously had allowed South Africa to field a team for Davis Cup play the following year. "A more cynical man than I might think that I was a quid pro quo [part of a deal]."[2] South Africa confirmed the deal, and Ashe wrote that he had assumed all along that the South African government "would use me in some way."[3]

A number of people—black and white, American and foreign, inside and outside tennis circles—did not want Ashe to go. He would, they said, be a tool of the racist government's propaganda. Ashe had decided to go long before he received acceptance. The South African Open was a very big contest each year, and Ashe very badly wanted to play. But more important, he was incredibly curious. Could

South Africa be as bad as he had heard? What was a modern, racist society really like? "I'm human," he said. "I just want to see the damn place with my own eyes and my own mind."[4]

He left for Johannesburg on the night of November 16, 1973, departing London on a British jetliner. On the way, Ashe went over in his mind just how important this breakthrough invitation really was. Television, he recalled, was virtually banned in South Africa. The government's thinking, evidently, was to hold "back the tide of human communications from its blacks by denying television to everyone. Thus, the whole land focuses heavily on major sporting events," such as the tournament in which he would play.[5]

Arriving at 3:45 the following morning, Ashe and several tennis officials and journalists were ushered toward a news conference. Ashe had agreed not to make any inflammatory statements while in the country, though on departure he insisted on speaking his mind. He also demanded that public seating for the tournament be opened equally to fans of all races. A news conference went smoothly, and several white South Africans wished Ashe luck in the tournament. Not all white South Africans supported the apartheid government.

Arthur stayed in the home of a wealthy businessperson. It was a sprawling, spacious, Spanish-style ranch, so large there was plenty of room in just one wing for Ashe and several others connected with the tourney. The tennis star was stunned when he asked for a cool drink, and the black African maid said, "Yes, master," and went to fetch it. He realized how far he had come, and he laughed almost wickedly as he thought: "So here is little Artie Ashe, the skinny black kid from the capital of the old Confederacy, all set up in a mansion, carrying on jes' like the white folks, and gettin' hisself called Master."[6]

Later on, at a reception, "everyone was just lovely to me."[7] And despite the fact that it was illegal for a white person to serve a black person alcohol, the get-together was sponsored by a brewery and was attended by persons from various ethnic and racial backgrounds. It was only later in the evening that Ashe realized the time—10 P.M., the curfew for all of the country's nonwhites. The following morning, his mood became more somber as he saw the number of "WHITES ONLY" signs posted on everything from toilets to drinking fountains. He put such matters temporarily out of mind and concentrated on getting used to the Johannesburg altitude. The city is five hundred feet higher than Denver, Colorado, for example, and the air is quite thin.

An observant person, the more Ashe looked around, the more he saw. Only black residents of the country were forced to carry passbooks signed by their white bosses. These books accounted for their time. If they were on a public street when the passbook said they should be at home or at work, they could be jailed. Even more distressing, there were informers of all races, everywhere. Persons who were arrested but not imprisoned could be banned, "which permits you to exist but not really to live," Ashe reported.[8]

Banning prevented a person from attending college, visiting a library, traveling, or even meeting more than one person at a time.

The suspicious nature of the South African government was seen firsthand during Ashe's visit. Without warning, the regime declared that blacks and other nonwhite South Africans could not compete against each other in amateur sports. A group of black journalists clustered around Ashe, but when he began to chat with them, fear crept across their faces. They urged him to invite them into the tennis clubhouse, an area where they felt they would not be overheard. One journalist gave Ashe details of his life in the country and was banned a few days later.

The air of fright and suspicion was not just in the mind of Arthur Ashe. Bud Collins, a Boston sportswriter who had also covered tennis for television, provided this view:

> There was something in the local air...that you didn't want to breathe: hate, oppression, cruelty. Evil. Even if you were a white visitor, unhassled, you couldn't be comfortable in this police state. Especially if you were white, and paying attention, you realized that South Africa wasn't as bad as you'd imagined and read about. It was worse.[9]

After winning his first match—against an American, Sherwood Steward—Ashe decided to visit all-black Soweto. The name sounds exotic, but Ashe learned it was an abbreviation for "Southwest Township." He presumed it was on the edge of Johannesburg but found it was seventeen miles away. Each day, thousands of black South African workers rode buses and trains into and out of the city. The government owned all housing in Soweto, which at the time of Ashe's visit held 1 million residents. There was one fire brigade, one hospital, and one switchboard for five hundred phones. The worst houses were tiny shacks of paper, wood, and tin. After a brief glimpse from a car, Ashe returned to Johannesburg.

But Ashe did not escape close contact with black South Africa. At a conference arranged by a banned journalist, nervous blacks called him an Uncle Tom—meaning a servant of the white man. Several of them told him and all other black Americans to stay away. Their visits, said the black South Africans, delayed the struggle for equality. Others urged the United States to boycott their apartheid country. Ashe admitted that South Africa was even more of a struggle than the United States had been for black people. But he told his somewhat hostile audience they were making progress. As it turned out, Ashe was not only correct but would live to see a free South Africa.

Back on the court, Ashe easily beat an Australian who had moved to South Africa. Eyeing the stands, he quickly saw that most nonwhites were being herded into seating around the edges of the court. High in one corner, a tight knot of black South Africans cheered for him wildly. He acknowledged their noise with a nod, aware that there were as many fans rooting against him as with him. He felt, he told Bud Collins, as if he were "walking a tightrope."[10]

"Arthur's playing well, and I don't know how he plays at all," said Jimmy Connors, a fellow American tennis pro. "There's so much emotion for him."[11] That emotion stayed hidden during his next match, which was with South African Cliff Drysdale. The country's best player, Drysdale had been so outspoken against racial policies that he eventually moved to the United States and became an American citizen. But on the day he and Ashe played in the semifinal in Johannesburg, the crowd seemed to be pulling equally for both players. Ashe won easily.

True to form, Ashe kept his emotions inside him. He returned to Soweto in the midst of the big tennis tournament to put on a tennis exhibition. Playing on the township's best court—there were only about twenty courts for 1 million people—Ashe felt as if he had accomplished something simply because so few outsiders ever came to Soweto to see it. In fact, most white residents of Johannesburg had never laid eyes on the place. After the clinic, Ashe autographed the dreaded passbooks as young residents of the immense ghetto either screamed, "Go home, leave us alone," or called "God bless you, Arthur."[12]

Back in the city of almost 1.9 million, Ashe had a sizeable task on his hands—to win the South African tournament he had to defeat fellow American Jimmy Connors. Much younger than Ashe, who was thirty, Connors was at the peak of his career. Though Ashe used his backhand well and handled the Connors serve, he nevertheless lost in three sets. "They will have to wait another year for a black man to be champion of South Africa," he decided.[13] That was not quite true. The following day, Ashe and Tom Okker of the Netherlands won the doubles championship in four sets over Australians Rob Maud and Lew Hoad.

Before departing the country, Ashe met with a college professor and his students who were of Afrikaner, or African-Dutch descent. Defenders of apartheid, they were quick to point out the many flaws with the United States, wondering if the United States had any business criticizing their form of government. Ashe agreed that the United States was beset by problems but noted that rioting and protesting are small prices to pay for freedom of expression. Even more important, Ashe got the Afrikaners to admit that freedom for only about 15 percent of the people in a country is indefensible.[14]

It was with a sense of satisfaction that Ashe climbed on the aircraft that would take him out of Africa. He told himself that those who criticized him for going to South Africa were wrong in their assessment of the situation. He also believed that it was just a matter of time until the apartheid system cracked and fell apart.[15] History has proven him correct—the white minority government in 1990 lifted its ban on the African National Congress (ANC), the black majority political party. National elections in April 1994 swept Nelson Mandela of the ANC into the presidency. Among many other benefits, black South Africans were no longer confined to certain limited geographical areas. They have become full-fledged citizens of the country.

Chapter 7

A WORLD-CLASS PLAYER

Not only was Arthur Ashe a very good tennis player, he was very good for a very long time. Giving him some benefit of the doubt, he was the best player in the United States during the decade from 1965 to 1975. In a sport where high-strung athletes are not usually at the peak of their game for more than a year or two, Ashe had real staying power.

Though some players gave him more trouble than others, it is safe to say that he beat everyone he played at one time or another. Some caused him difficulty. "Rocket" Rod Laver, the Australian, whipped Ashe dozens of times, yet the American managed to beat Laver twice. Others, such as America's Roscoe Tanner, said to have the world's fastest serve, sometimes caused him problems. But he held his own against rising, current, and fading stars from all over the world.

And because there was money behind open tennis, Ashe played all across the globe, becoming known on every continent. Despite the demands of constant travel, he continued to stay involved in the players' association and in doing a good deed when and where possible. One of his good deeds took place in Africa during a tennis tour in the French-speaking Cameroons.

Ashe was at a tennis club and saw an eleven-year-old boy playing there who may have reminded the Virginia native of himself at a similar age. He offered the boy one of his own gleaming metal rackets for a few minutes of play. Ashe was so impressed with the child's ability that he contacted the boy's father and arranged for him to be taught tennis in France. The boy would grow up to be Yannick Noah, winner of the French title in 1983.

Ashe bobbed around at the top of the ever-changing world rankings for quite some time. In 1973, for example, he was ranked tenth, a false indication that his best days were behind him. Two years later, Ashe topped all players in official earnings, having won $326,750—twice as much as Jimmy Connors. His play in open tennis resulted in Ashe winning a total of thirty-three titles and being the losing finalist thirty-two times. He won against such giants of the game as Guillermo Vilas, Bjorn Borg, Ilie Nastase, Manuel Orantes, and, of course, Jimmy Connors.[1]

Going into the Wimbledon matches in the summer of 1975, no one gave Ashe much of a chance. Connors, after all, had failed to win only two tournaments in the previous six months—an astounding record. But Ashe may have decided he was the best grass player never to have won at Wimbledon, and that it was his turn. All eyes were on Connors, who loved to return powerful shots even faster than they were hit to him. He thrived on ball speed, coming toward him and flying back across the net. Since Ashe was a power player, could he ever hope to win?

The first thing Ashe did that year at Wimbledon was beat Bjorn Borg. He was the last person to defeat the superb Swedish player for six years at Wimbledon. But to beat Jimmy Connors, Ashe would have to try something different. Consulting his coach, Dennis Ralston, he decided for the only time in his entire career to alter his game. Walking onto center court on a warm, overcast afternoon, Ashe later told reporters that he firmly believed he could win.[2] Few fans felt the same way.

Those who anticipated rocketlike shots from Ashe were in for a surprise. Except for his serves, which were as quick as always, Ashe went for precision instead of speed. He softly returned Connors' shots, placing them just out of reach of the snorting, sweating, younger opponent. Ashe took the first two sets six games to one, and the crowd was stunned. No one had ever beaten

Connors by much, yet the thirty-one-year-old Ashe was demolishing the rising star before their very eyes. Ashe needed to win a third set to take home the cup.

Ashe relied frequently that day on the lob, a high, soft shot meant to go over his opponent's head. He used the shot effectively several times, then surprised Connors with pinpoint forehands—shots that were considered the weakest part of the African American's game. Though Connors did manage to win one set, Ashe won the fourth set, 6-4. The championship at Wimbledon was his. At the press conference that followed, he said, "I felt it was my destiny."[3]

Few players could have altered the way they played the game overnight. It took tremendous discipline not to smash the ball or go for the tricky shot, as Ashe had always done. Instead, he simply tried to play a game that was error free. It worked.

Ashe could have been called the thinking person's tennis player. Not because he was obsessive about tennis but because he was an addicted reader, learning about issues and getting personally involved. That was true of the Association of Tennis Professionals he helped form, and it was true of numerous human-rights causes. Throughout his career he gave time and talent to several charities.

But the lanky African American could have a good time. He enjoyed drinking beer with fellow tennis pros, particularly the always-cheerful Australians. And he liked women. During one memorable series of tournaments in Europe, a lovely Jamaican woman was seen with Ashe in a number of countries. Nevertheless, he did not get serious about any woman in particular until 1976.

The tennis star was in New York City for a United Negro College Fund benefit. He noticed a striking young woman with a camera and learned that her name was Jeanne-Marie Moutoussamy. A Chicago native, she worked for NBC as a graphic artist and was working on her skills as a professional photographer. Ashe introduced himself and the two engaged in small talk. After a four-month courtship, they were married on Feb. 20, 1977.

Though neither Mr. nor Mrs. Ashe ever said so, the next two years proved to be very happy ones. The tennis pro and the photographer were mature enough to enjoy the monetary rewards of their work—the couple jetted off to Europe for a tennis tourney one week, then spent the next week relaxing at a Florida golf resort or amid the solitude of a crystal-clear lake in upstate New York.

In 1978, Ashe completed his tenth year as a member of America's Davis Cup team. As the decade neared its end, he was experienced, known and admired around the world, and had few tennis goals remaining. He assumed he would play professionally for a few more years, then combine business, activism, and leisure, living with Jeanne in New York City.[4]

On July 30, 1979, a week after competing in a tournament in Austria, Ashe awoke late one night with terrible chest pain. He was in his New York apartment, sleeping alongside his wife, and all had seemed well. He shrugged off the pain as indigestion and tried to go back to sleep. It went away, only to return within minutes. Ashe again convinced himself it was only an upset stomach and tried to put it out of his mind.[5]

At a tennis clinic nearby the following day, the pain returned. Fortunately, a physician was playing on a nearby court. He questioned Ashe, suspected that the tennis star had suffered a heart attack, and personally took him to a hospital. The thirty-six-year-old tennis pro spent the next two days in intensive care, followed by eight more days in the hospital's coronary (heart-care) area. Doctors confirmed that he had suffered a heart attack, adding that he would never play tennis again unless he had surgery.

"Because I did not want my career to end in 1979, on December 13 of that year I underwent a quadruple coronary bypass operation," Ashe wrote in his best-selling memoir, *Days of Grace*.[6] The operation involved opening Ashe's chest, sawing through his breastbone, and spreading apart his ribs to reach his heart. Using veins from the tennis star's legs, the surgeon bypassed clogged arteries to restore a healthy blood flow to the heart. The operation appeared successful, though no one promised Ashe that he could return to tennis.

Less than three months later, Ashe was vacationing in Cairo, Egypt. On the afternoon of March 9, 1980, he left his hotel to exercise. As he broke into a run, heart pains similar to the ones he felt in 1979 pulsed through his chest. He immediately stopped running and walked slowly back to the hotel. An American doctor and friend who had joined the Ashes on the vacation checked Ashe over and told him to return to New York. The Virginia native's long career in professional tennis was over.

Chapter 8

A SHOCKING END TO TENNIS

Arthur received medication and advice from top physicians, and the care allowed him to captain America's Davis Cup team from 1981 to 1985. The former star directed cup wins in 1981 and 1982. Despite his health, Ashe craved the "great honor and responsibility" of serving as captain.[1]

This was courageous in view of the fact that Ashe underwent a second heart-bypass operation in 1983. Veins from other parts of his body were used to bypass two of his clogged arteries. One result of the operation was that Ashe lost a quantity of blood; the blood loss made him feel queasy immediately following the operation. A doctor told him he would rebuild slowly, but that a blood transfusion would make him feel better immediately. Ashe asked for the transfusion.

Ashe learned in 1981 that Captain Tony Trabert had grown tired of running the Davis Cup team. Trabert, a legendary player in the 1950s, hated the behavior of the new stars. Ashe was younger than Trabert and felt he might connect better with the players. Would the players appreciate his subtle approach, or would they run over him because he was too nice? Above all, Ashe wondered how he would work with John McEnroe, the brilliant yet explosive player who nevertheless felt it his duty to compete for the cup.

America's Davis Cup team needed all the help it could get. At the time Ashe assumed his leadership role, the team had won the title only two times in the previous five years. By way of comparison, the United States went undefeated in Davis Cup play for five straight years between 1968 and 1972. By the 1980s, terms such as "amateur" and "professional" had lost much of their meaning. Amateurs clawed their way into Davis Cup play, while professionals might play or avoid the tournament, according to their moods. One who usually dodged Davis Cup play was Jimmy Connors.

Connors was like Ashe in that he came from a modest background. Ashe approached Connors repeatedly to join the Davis Cup team, but he did not succeed until 1984. Even then, Connors was uncomfortable; John McEnroe clearly was the best American on the court. In fact, McEnroe was among the very best players ever to pick up a racket. A left-hander, he won his first major title as an eighteen-year-old amateur, startling tennis buffs at Wimbledon by making it to the semifinals as a rookie. What may have startled followers of tennis more than McEnroe's brilliant game was his thunderous temper. He and Ashe could not have been less alike.

Yet they sometimes got along. Ashe appreciated the string of Davis Cup wins McEnroe had put together, doing well as an individual and as a doubles partner even when other team members were soundly defeated. McEnroe would become the only American to play on more Davis Cup teams than Ashe. Through 1992, he had competed twelve years.

In his first Davis Cup tournament, Ashe chose to play McEnroe in singles, but not in doubles. McEnroe won his first big match, but Roscoe Tanner lost. Ashe received some timely advice from Richard Gonzales, one of America's legendary tennis greats. Gonzales told Ashe the theory about not mixing singles and doubles players was a bad one, especially when singles players were as capable as McEnroe. Ashe took the veteran's advice, and the Americans mowed through the field.

Equally important, Gonzales told the Davis Cup coach that he looked too nonchalant on the sidelines. Ashe protested that he got so caught up in some matches that he could feel his heart race.

"Well, we don't want your heart to thump too much," Gonzales said with a smile, aware of Ashe's medical history. "But you have to *look* more involved, I guess."[2]

Involvement became a sore point with Ashe during his years as the Davis Cup captain. He could recall that some players, such as Roscoe Tanner, enjoyed his advice. Others resented it. Ashe was sensitive to the fact that many of America's best players did not want to be instructed in front of thousands of fans and millions of television viewers. Ashe also had no intention of joining his players when they argued with officials.[3]

McEnroe threw tantrums at Wimbledon while defeating Bjorn Borg in 1981 for the men's singles title, and it cost him $2,250 in fines. For the first time in history, Wimbledon administrators refused to grant him membership, which they had always done for previous winners. Ashe wondered how McEnroe would behave in Davis Cup play. McEnroe lost to Ivan Lendl as Jimmy Connors demolished Tomas Smid. McEnroe then beat Smid and Connors beat Lendl. The cup was back in American hands.

Ashe sensed that Connors might not play in future Davis Cup matches, but he said nothing. After all, he had criticized Connors for not playing in 1975, and Connors had filed suit against Ashe, complaining of libel. (After Ashe beat Connors at Wimbledon that year for the singles title, the suit was dropped.) Ashe was equally concerned about McEnroe, who could be counted on to represent his country in the Davis Cup, but who hated all authority—even Ashe when he was serving as captain.

Captain and player had their biggest clash in 1984 Davis Cup play. The site was Cincinnati, Ohio, where John McEnroe and Peter Fleming were opposed by Argentines

Guillermo Vilas and Jose Luis Clerc. The Argentines teased, stalled, and otherwise infuriated McEnroe. At one point, the four players came at each other, separated by nothing but the net. Ashe rushed onto the court and ordered McEnroe away from the confrontation. The two exchanged bitter words. Ashe actually thought he might lose control of himself and punch his best player. He was certainly testing his health—a year earlier, Ashe had undergone his second heart-bypass surgery. McEnroe and Fleming pulled themselves together and won the match.

But Ashe was not through. He quickly placed several long-distance calls to ensure that he had the support of Davis Cup officials. Early the next morning, he and McEnroe met. They spoke carefully to each other, Ashe warning the star that, if McEnroe misbehaved in that day's match, the United States would default.

McEnroe kept his temper in check the following day, beating Clerc in five sets. Looking back on that time, Ashe noted that McEnroe's outrage was as noisy as Ashe's was contained. Ashe believed that he might have been a bit envious toward McEnroe for being able to explode on court, getting all of his complaints out of his system.[4] What would have happened if people like Arthur Ashe, Sr., Ron Charity, and Robert Johnson had allowed their star to scream at an opponent or make rude gestures to the crowd?

Ashe said:

I developed a deep affection for McEnroe, and also a genuine respect for his character and integrity that defused my outrage at behavior so different from my own. What bound me to McEnroe was not simply his rage but also his selflessness in making sacrifices to play for our country, and his artistry on the tennis court. I couldn't resist that combination.[5]

Ashe's Davis Cup career came to an end in October 1985, a few months after he was inducted into the International Tennis Hall of Fame. Davis Cup officials felt Ashe should be replaced. The former star was neither surprised nor upset at the decision, feeling that he failed to force players to behave. He also "accepted the fact that as much as I want to lead others, and love to be around other people, in some essential way I am something of a loner."[6]

He also knew that his increasing activism—which had included protests and an occasional arrest—in opposition to the conservative administration of President Ronald Reagan made tennis officials nervous. He may have been aware, too, that the Davis Cup job, though it did not take up all twelve months of each year, was a grueling one on someone who has had heart-bypass surgery.

Chapter 9

DOING WELL

Ashe was not sure what other athletes did after their playing and coaching days, but he knew he could not be idle. He had made a great deal of money as a professional tennis star, allowing him a plush apartment in New York City and two vacation homes. He chose to remain busy, even though his name no longer flashed regularly worldwide on radio or television, or in the newspapers.

Ashe had always been good at sharing his views, so demand for him as a speaker continued. Most present and retired athletes used agents to arrange their speaking dates. Ashe did the arranging himself, accepting low pay if he especially liked his audience or was asked to speak on subjects dear to his heart. His ability impressed Yale University, a famous Ivy League school, and he was offered a position as a lecturer there.

The former tennis star was thrilled by the honor.[1] But after a great deal of thought, he declined. Instead, he decided to teach at Florida Memorial College. Known as FMC, it had only twelve hundred students. All were African Americans, few were from well-to-do families, and most were from the Miami area. In 1985, Ashe taught a course at FMC he called "The Black Athlete in Contemporary Society."

Prior to the first class meeting, Ashe went looking for histories of African-American athletes. Although there have been thousands of African Americans who played all sorts of sports, information was hard to find. Ashe realized with a shock that many great African-American baseball players, boxers, and track stars had faded from almost everyone's memory. He set out to do something about that.

Ashe found only two books on the subject. One was almost fifty years old. Leafing through the pages of these two sports histories, Ashe came upon truly world-class athletes that were all but unknown. For example, most early Kentucky Derby jockeys were African American. But they were forgotten. There was Josh Gibson, an early baseball player who hit at least as far and as well as Babe Ruth. There was Marshall Taylor, a champion cyclist. And there was George Poage, the first African American to win an Olympic medal. Clearly, hundreds of past athletes deserved to be remembered.

Ashe had written earlier books, but nothing this ambitious. He hired an assistant to help him organize the mass of material, and he used other editors and researchers. Before the manuscript took final form, he had spent $300,000. *A Hard Road to Glory: A History of the African-American Athlete* came out in 1988. It was a three-volume set that covered African Americans in sports from 1619 to 1985. Today, the work is an important reference in school and public libraries.

Meanwhile, Ashe began to work for the first time with his FMC students, covering a fascinating subject. The students seemed interested, and all went well until, two or three weeks into the course, Ashe made a brief written assignment. He collected the papers, looked them over, and was so upset that "my hands shook with disbelief and anger the first time I read their prose."[2]

Except for three women students who had handed in excellent work, the remaining papers were terrible. Words were misspelled or used incorrectly, there was no sense of organization, and the writers reached no conclusions. Ashe graded the papers at the dining-room table of his vacation home near Miami, becoming more depressed with each passing minute. Were the former tennis star's expectations too high?

Ashe sought answers from a Florida Memorial College administrator, also an African-American male. What he heard did little to improve his mood. The administrator believed that disadvantaged African-American students must be given a break in view of how difficult growing up black in the United States really was. Teachers at the college were to show students there was a better way to do things rather than simply flunk those who could not do the work, Ashe was told.[3]

Ashe pondered the administrator's words. The former tennis star had always made good grades, and he had grown up under segregation—what was wrong with young people today? They were treated better by whites, yet results were dismal. Gradually, Ashe came to realize that he had been separated from average students almost from the start. Even in grade school, he and other gifted African-American children were grouped together and taught more and better than most other children, whatever their color.

The former athlete sympathized with his students, yet he decided to hold their work to his own high standards. One by one, the students dropped his class. Ashe worried about those unable to do the work.[4] But he had little patience for students who showed up late for class, forgot assignments, or asked too many simple questions. The semester was a tough one for Ashe, but from it came several of his most deeply held convictions.

He believed that African-American colleges were an important part of African-American culture. Surely, if these colleges did not preserve African-American history, no one else would. Ashe boosted the amount of money he gave each year to the United Negro College Fund, which raises funds for most African-American schools. And he began a campaign for higher academic standards for athletes at all colleges and universities.[5]

Not all of Ashe's time was devoted to righting the wrongs of the world. On December 21, 1986, Mr. and Mrs. Ashe became the parents of a baby daughter. Jeanne's pregnancy had been a time of both hope and concern, since heart disease was present on both sides of the family. But Camera, as their daughter was named, was born not only healthy but beautiful. The first-time parents hovered over her for months, overjoyed at her presence.

With plenty of money and a loving family, why did Arthur Ashe exert himself? With wealth and other advantages, little Camera probably would grow to be a top student. Ashe was interested in the future of each and every African American—particularly those who had little or no money and who were gifted athletes.

Digging for information, he was shocked to learn that only about one male athlete in four—black or white—graduates from the college he enters. What did this tell him? Primarily, it said that colleges were more interested in the athlete's body than in his mind. Was there a connection between the decline of classroom performance by African Americans and the "Black Power" movement of the 1960s?

Black Power was born of impatience. Young African Americans had heard Dr. Martin Luther King, Jr., and others preach nonviolence for years. By 1965, they were fed up with turning the other cheek. Led by activists such as Stokely Carmichael (now Kwame Toure), the Black Power movement was born. It told blacks that the white majority owed them for decades of slavery and segregation.

Ashe was no saint. He believed that African Americans should grab all the power they could hold. But the former Wimbledon winner felt that Black Power had turned its back on morality. African Americans, he believed, had moved from morality and liberation to hatred and violence.

The attitude Black Power created in young African Americans came between them and success, Ashe felt. It did exactly what it tried not to do—create failure. Blacks now found failure something they could blame on the white majority. Ashe found that Black Power belittled knowledge and discipline, tools successful African Americans had always used.

An offshoot of this movement was the insistence that African Americans should be taught courses about their culture. Consequently, they learned less about business or economics or writing and more about black culture—in a society where they were less than 15 percent of the population. Worse, black students who studied hard and made good grades were belittled by friends.

Ashe learned a great deal about the state of African-American education by teaching at Florida Memorial College. But he learned even more during the national debate in the 1980s over how smart a college athlete needs to be. This controversy involved the National Collegiate Athletic Association (NCAA) and how colleges selected student athletes.

The NCAA had come under fire because there were athletes in colleges who could barely read or write. Was it fair to admit a poor student when better-qualified students might be turned down? Equally important, was it fair to student athletes to use them and then send them home without skills or education? What was the right thing to do?

Like most things, Ashe had strong feelings about this nationwide question. Since most athletes who played football or basketball or ran track at large colleges were African Americans, there were racial overtones to any discussion about grades, test scores, intelligence, and African Americans. When the NCAA changed admission rules, the discussion became more heated.

According to the National Collegiate Athletic Association, a freshman could play for one of the 277 top athletic schools only if he earned a C average in high school. Equally important, that student had to have studied English, mathematics, social studies, and physical sciences in high school, and achieve a certain level on national entrance examinations.

Ashe believed the requirements "should present no challenge whatsoever even to the average student."[6] Many people felt otherwise, including several black and white college presidents. They called the new standards racist, even though they applied equally to all college freshmen. Others opposed to higher standards included the National Association for the Advancement of Colored People (NAACP), the Reverend Jesse Jackson, and the National Baptist Convention.

Ashe's views proved unpopular. He wrote a letter to *The New York Times*, challenging college presidents to make education more important than sports to all students. He also published arguments in *Ebony* magazine, and he visited African-American high schools to tell students there what would be expected of them under the new rules. Ashe picked up an ally in Joe Paterno, the legendary Pennsylvania State University football coach, who warned against overemphasizing athletics. He also attracted at least two powerful and respected foes.

John Thompson, the basketball coach at Georgetown University, and John Chaney, the Temple University coach, are both African Americans. Thompson told Ashe in a telephone conversation that the new rules might benefit society, but they would result in fewer African Americans admitted to colleges. He also believed admissions tests were culturally biased—that is, they were tilted in favor of common knowledge among white students and away from common knowledge among black students.

Ashe felt that any loss in the number of African-American college students would be a brief one. He was convinced that African-American high school students would learn of the new rules and boost their classroom work to meet them. Ashe agreed with Chaney that African Americans "deserve a chance," but he felt everyone deserved a chance and no one should be granted special favors.[7]

The tennis star was pleased the NCAA imposed tougher rules. He was just as pleased to see affirmative action, a government program, begin to be questioned at about the same time. Affirmative action allows minorities slightly better access to jobs and other opportunities than the white majority to make up for past discrimination. Ashe argued that affirmative action hurt the people it was designed to help, keeping them mediocre.

Ashe had other disagreements with much of the black community. He questioned the early teachings of Malcolm X, the late activist who dreamed of a separate black nation for African Americans under the religion of Islam. Ashe deeply respected Dr. Martin Luther King, Jr., but pointed out that, since the deaths of Malcolm X and King, there were few younger African-American leaders on the horizon.

Why did Ashe care about any of this? And if he cared so deeply, why did he not assume a leadership role? He served as a member of the board of directors of Aetna, a major insurance company, and he was asked to think about running for Congress but declined. Ashe wanted what was best for the country. But he was an African American, too, and he wanted what was best for his people. His aim was to make African Americans competitive off the playing field. African Americans, as *A Hard Road to Glory* indicated, had nothing left to prove in sports. But there were other areas that cried out for improvement, and Ashe ached to see signs of real progress.[8]

Chapter 10

THE SURGEON'S DISCOVERY

For about five years following the second heart-bypass operation, Arthur Ashe lived a healthy—though no longer athletic—life. He had no idea he was HIV-positive—that the AIDS virus lay dormant inside him. His painful awareness of AIDS began on a sunny summer morning in 1988. The Ashes were on vacation, this time at an exclusive resort on Lake George in upstate New York. Ashe awoke unable to fully use the fingers on his left hand. They were not numb, and there was no pain. Nevertheless, he had to ask Jeanne to dial a phone number for him. By the time the Ashes checked out of the resort, Ashe's left hand hung helplessly by his side.

He quickly saw his family doctor when he got home. Though no specialist, the doctor realized immediately that the normal signals being sent from the brain were not reaching the hand. He knew of no other reason for the hand to quit working.

Ashe wanted to get to the bottom of the problem and, believing he might have had a stroke, took a series of tests. They revealed a small, mysterious mass on the left side of the retired tennis star's brain. The only sure way to tell what the mass might be was a biopsy—surgeons penetrated Ashe's skull, removing the small mass. Ashe awoke quickly and felt much better than during the periods following his earlier heart surgeries. But he was soon stunned to learn from physicians that the mass was an indication that he had AIDS. "Not only was I HIV-positive; I had full-blown AIDS," Ashe thought to himself.[1]

His first concern was that he might have infected Jeanne or little Camera, his daughter, who was just twenty-one months old at the time. Happily, both later were tested and proved to be HIV-negative. Despite the fact that several people within the hospital knew of Ashe and the disease, Arthur and Jeanne decided to keep the problem to themselves. They did so for several reasons, among them consideration for their daughter and for Ashe's aging father. Ashe felt that additional bad news about his health might be more than the old man's weak heart could bear.[2]

The mass in his brain, which was safely removed, was an AIDS-related infection called toxoplasmosis. Many people carry the virus around inside them, but the disease only seems to blossom inside the bodies of those whose immune systems are battered by AIDS. Several other diseases might strike Ashe at any time: a deadly form of pneumonia, a cancer called Kaposi's sarcoma, meningitis, diarrhea, tuberculosis, and more. Unfortunately for Ashe and about thirteen thousand others nationwide, they received transfusions which contained the virus before widespread testing to detect the disease was used on the blood supply.

Ashe had always been a voracious reader, so he began to gather information about his illness. He learned, for example, that suicide among AIDS patients was about six times the expected rate. But Ashe felt that committing suicide—or even becoming severely depressed—was surrendering to the disease. Equally important, it would have hurt his family and friends. Ashe first attended church in his infancy, and he began to lean on his Christianity more and more as the days passed. A skeptic as a child and a virtual nonbeliever as a young adult, Ashe had come to see religion's value even before he learned of his disease.

Others took refuge in religion on Ashe's behalf. Immediately after telling the public that he had AIDS, people from all across the country wrote to him, telling him he was in their prayers. Others suggested treatments of all sorts, perhaps unaware that Ashe already was being treated with the best conventional medicines available. Some of them virtually guaranteed cures, often telling of powerful herbal teas and other organic remedies for all sorts of afflictions. And though Ashe wondered if suppressing his emotions might have made him catch the disease more easily, he decided to put himself completely in the hands of his New York physicians.

The physicians had their hands full. For example, Ashe had always been allergic to penicillin, the powerful antibiotic. So he was given a different germ-killer, this one sulfur-derived, and the sulfur crystallized in his system, producing kidney stones. Later, his entire body reacted to the powerful chemical, leaving his skin temporarily disfigured and swelling his mouth with painful sores. With long periods of bed rest prescribed, Ashe read all he could find about his disease. An article in *Scientific American* indicated that most AIDS patients live an average of only three years after being diagnosed. How long, Ashe wondered, did he still have?

He could not bring himself to ask that question aloud. Instead, he tried to become the ideal patient, taking every pill exactly on schedule and getting the exact amounts of rest, exercise, and food suggested by physicians. He agreed to take AZT, the powerful and controversial anti-AIDS drug, even though it had been rushed into production so quickly that it had not been as thoroughly tested as many other drugs on the market. By 1992, Ashe was taking $18,000 worth of pills a year—some thirty a day, every day. Despite all the medicine, he developed sores in his mouth known as thrush, and he suffered from almost chronic diarrhea.

Ashe put an optimistic spin on his condition in 1992: "With AIDS, I have good days and bad days. The good days, thank goodness, greatly outnumber the bad. And the bad days are not unendurable."[3] He rejected the belief that such terrible afflictions as AIDS are God's way of punishing homosexuals and drug users, a point made clear by the number of hemophiliacs, whom, like Ashe, had been infected by transfusion.

Sadly, physical problems mounted in 1993. The Ashe family had spent the week following Christmas at the Doral resort in Florida. Ashe was playing a round of golf, a game he had learned to enjoy, on New Year's Day. Although he was riding from shot to shot in a golf cart, he noticed that his breathing became gradually labored. Equipped with a cellular phone, Arthur called his AIDS physician from the course and was told to see a doctor as quickly as possible. He learned a few days later that one of the arteries leading to his heart was virtually closed. But there was more bad news: His lungs were causing the acute shortness of breath and the wrenching cough that went with it.

His body temperature rising, Ashe popped some acetaminophen, bundled himself and his family, and caught a plane back to New York City. Ashe's physician examined him and, believing he had a form of pneumonia, gave him a powerful antibiotic. The drug had no effect. Specialists pushed a tube down the AIDS victim's throat, at the end of which was a tiny camera. The view confirmed not only that Ashe had pneumonia but that it was the most dreaded form, commonly found in those afflicted with his disease. Ashe took little comfort in being told he would survive the bout of pneumonia because his fever continued to rage, showing that his body was fighting the illness.

Ashe began very slowly to recover from pneumonia in a swanky hospital room once used by John F. Kennedy. From his bed he had a sweeping view of the New York City skyline. Without the constant ringing of the phone, he had a bit of time to think back over his life. The things that mattered to him—friends, family, books, all kinds of music—still mattered. But as he sensed that his life was approaching its end, he took refuge in the teachings of Howard Thurman. An African American who blended many theologies, Thurman's writing helped Ashe accept the pain he had suffered, as an African American and as an AIDS victim, and the pain he would continue to undergo.[4]

The tennis star with the fragile health said he never asked himself, "Why me?" If he were to ask that question of his burdens, would he not also have to ask it of his blessings? How many African-American children in Richmond, Virginia, had been blessed with a strong, capable father, a large, extended family, and a diligent coach who took the time to teach Ashe not only about tennis but about life itself? Ashe wrote that he did not pray to be granted favors but to find out what God might have in store for him. He refused to pray to be rid of either the diseased heart or of the AIDS virus.[5]

Ashe did not fear death, but he was not sure why. If he was into denial, it was based on his refusal to dwell on the fact that his life would soon end. Each night, whether with his family or in a hospital bed, he simply lay down and went to sleep. His thoughts plunged through current affairs, political and social activism, giving of his time, his friends, his family, and his religion. Aside from the fact that he was dying, he felt blessed.[6]

Ironically, AIDS was not the heaviest burden of Arthur Ashe's life. Rather, it was the whole matter of race. Ashe said he came to this realization while talking with a reporter for *People* magazine who had interviewed him in 1992 shortly after he went public with details of his battle with AIDS.[7] When readers found out about his views, they created quite a stir.

An African-American radio station in Chicago presented a lively call-in debate on Ashe's feelings over the air. Others called and wrote to Ashe, wondering if he had been misquoted. No, he reported sadly, he had not. In fact, he told those who inquired, being of African heritage in America was a complex thing. To emphasize the effect it had on him, he said, "I . . . sometimes think that this indeed may be one of those fates that are worse than death."[8]

Not everyone agreed with the popular celebrity. Was this any kind of message to send to young African Americans, people who eagerly awaited adulthood and were optimistic about the future? Ashe contended that he was an optimist himself—no easy thing to be with AIDS slowly destroying his body's immune system. But he felt "a pall of sadness" dangle over not only his life but the lives of all African Americans because of what he and his people had experienced.[9]

Unfortunately, not all such experiences were in the past. Every day, African Americans are subjected to people and events, large and small, that conspire to weigh them down. A black man walks down the street and watches as whites fearfully cross the street to avoid him. A black woman who is pregnant often is seen as being automatically unmarried.

The shadow of race was first cast upon Ashe in his segregated hometown. The rules imposed on African Americans were, they were told, designed to make them "separate but equal" citizens. As anyone could tell, things were usually separate but seldom equal. For example, public rest rooms that were labeled for use by African Americans were not well maintained. When blacks complained about rest room conditions, the whites who were in power told them the facilities had been equal but black misuse was responsible for the inferior conditions. In one brief statement, white city fathers shifted the blame, making blacks responsible for their inferior positions in life.

Breakthroughs by African Americans in several important areas, overcoming enormous odds, helped snap the stranglehold of segregation. Besides athletic pioneers such as Jackie Robinson in baseball and Wilt Chamberlain in basketball, there were people such as Edward Brooke of Massachusetts, the first United States senator of African descent. Each year, more and more African-American entertainers were seen on television. Yet the largest strides were made by African-American musicians, whose wonderful sound captured the hearts and minds of both black and white young in America and around the world in the 1950s and 1960s. It seemed that the only people better known than sports stars during Ashe's college years were James Brown, Marvin Gaye, Smokey Robinson, Diana Ross, and dozens of other African-American talents, many of them familiar through the Motown record label.

Yet it was not the number of well-known African Americans, but the everyday people who were on Ashe's mind. In 1992, for example, while protesting America's policy of returning Haitian refugees, the former tennis star suffered his third heart attack. He was rushed to New York Hospital, a place that was familiar to him from earlier medical needs. Though preoccupied with his health, Ashe noticed that there were few blacks in positions of authority in the emergency room. In contrast, most of the people responsible for cleaning the floors were African Americans. Even though he was in ill health, race had once again entered his consciousness.[10]

Ashe tried to be objective about race. In his later years, he saw himself not as an African American or an American but something more. To emphasize such feelings, one of his proudest possessions was a simple T-shirt. Able to afford extravagant clothing, he nevertheless enjoyed pulling on the shirt, which displayed this inscription: "A citizen of the world."[11]

Chapter 11

A CITIZEN OF THE WORLD

Arthur Ashe died in a New York City hospital on February 6, 1993, of AIDS-related pneumonia. His body was returned to his hometown of Richmond for burial.

Though friends, acquaintances, health-care personnel, and the public knew he was dying, no one was prepared for the end. They all felt it had come too quickly, an assumption propped up by the fact that Ashe stayed mentally active until the end, telephoning his many friends and acquaintances from his hospital bed in order to share his views.

Arnold Rampersad, who met Ashe in 1992 at a children's book fair, worked with Ashe to complete his memoir, *Days of Grace*. The former star's health took a downward turn the last seven months of his life, the period of his association with Rampersad. The coauthor gazed in awe as Ashe remained friendly and cooperative while popping pills and enduring almost constant pain. The tennis legend answered letters and returned phone calls promptly from well-known persons and from those he had never met. How was he able to carry on? Because, Rampersad decided, he was at peace with himself.[1]

Not everyone was at peace over Ashe's death. Bryant Gumbel, the host of NBC-TV's morning *Today* show, showed viewers snapshots of the Ashe family relaxing at a picnic with the Gumbel family shortly before one of Ashe's many hospital stays. Gumbel usually hid his emotions almost as well as did Ashe, but he came apart in front of millions of television viewers.[2] So did many of those who knew Ashe, whether they were well known, such as Gumbel, or people like the elderly lady who lived next door to the tennis star when he was a globe-trotting bachelor. She saw him trudge in from tennis matches and set her teapot boiling. Ashe had delighted in having a quiet and relaxed cup of tea with his aging neighbor after hobnobbing with sports celebrities and the tennis-crazed public.

There were millions of others whose names would never be known but who would benefit from the presence of Arthur Ashe on Earth for forty-nine years. Among them were black South Africans, penned like cattle when Ashe visited them but given human rights shortly before the tennis star's death. His first visit to South Africa did not win universal approval among African blacks, but it was no coincidence that Nelson Mandela, the new black leader of South Africa, entertained Ashe in 1991 in Johannesburg and expressed joy at seeing Ashe again when Mandela paid the United States a visit in 1992.

At least as downtrodden as black South Africans were the Haitians in the 1990s. Ashe got himself arrested for protesting President George Bush's policy that returned Haitian immigrants to their dangerous and poverty-stricken homeland. Ashe had been placed under arrest before for his activism, which might have been one reason why Davis Cup officials relieved him of the duties of captain after the 1985 matches. But Ashe's activism may have played a part in President Bill Clinton's decision to send troops to Haiti in 1994 to restore democratic government.

It is fair to say that Ashe was most at home on the tennis court. So it was appropriate that Bud Collins, the sportswriter, dedicated his massive tennis encyclopedia "For the heroic Arthur Ashe, who showed us that sportsmanship even in a highly competitive game and world is a strength, not a weakness."[3]

CHRONOLOGY

1943—Arthur Ashe, Jr., is born on July 10 in Richmond, Virginia.

1953—Attends his first summer tennis camp at the Lynchburg, Virginia, home of Dr. Robert W. Johnson.

1960—Attends his final year of high school in St. Louis.

1961—Enters the University of California at Los Angeles (UCLA) on a scholarship; wins the national interscholastic tennis tournament.

1963—Plays in his first Davis Cup international competition;
–1978 continues to play Davis Cup matches for fifteen years, compiling a record of 27–5.

1965—Graduates from college with a degree in business administration and wins the national intercollegiate men's singles title.

1967—Serves in the United States Army as a second
–1969 lieutenant.

1968—Wins the U.S. Open while still an amateur player by beating Holland's Tom Okker.

1969—Discharged from the military and becomes a tennis professional.

1970—Wins the Australian men's singles tennis tournament.

1971—Wins the French doubles tennis tournament.

1972—Helps found the Association of Tennis Professionals.

1973—Makes a historic visit to South Africa, becoming the first black person to play in a major tennis tournament there.

1975—Against sizeable odds, beats Jimmy Connors to win Wimbledon.

1977—Marries Jeanne-Marie Moutoussamy; wins the Australian doubles title.

1979—Suffers a heart attack and undergoes heart-bypass surgery.

1981 –1978—Serves as captain of the United States Davis Cup team.

1983—Undergoes a second heart-bypass operation; following the operation, he receives a blood transfusion containing the HIV virus.

1987—Arthur and Jeanne Ashe become the parents of a daughter they name Camera.

1992—Forced by a newspaper's investigation to reveal that he has AIDS.

1993—Dies at the age of forty-nine on February 6 of an AIDS-related illness.

CHAPTER NOTES

Chapter 1. Publicity's Glare

1. Arthur Ashe and Arnold Rampersad, *Days of Grace* (New York: Alfred A. Knopf, 1993), p. 17.

2. Frank Deford, *Arthur Ashe*, Home Box Office television documentary, September 27, 1994.

3. Kenny Moore, "The Eternal Example," *Sports Illustrated*, December 21, 1992, pp. 16–27.

Chapter 2. Growing Up

1. Arthur Ashe and Arnold Rampersad, *Days of Grace* (New York: Alfred A. Knopf, 1993), p. 3.

2. Ibid., p. 50.

3. Ibid., p. 60.

4. John McPhee, *Levels of the Game* (New York: Farrar, Straus and Giroux, 1969), p. 29.

Chapter 3. A Strong Mentor

1. Arthur Ashe and Frank Deford, *Arthur Ashe: Portrait in Motion* (Boston: Houghton Mifflin, 1975), p. 29.

2. Ibid., p. 45.

3. Mary Huzinec et. al., "Man of Grace and Glory," *People Weekly*, February 22, 1993, p. 69.

4. Ashe and Deford, p. 94.

5. Ibid., p. 4.

6. Kenny Moore, "The Eternal Example," *Sports Illustrated*, December 21, 1992, p. 16.

7. John McPhee, *Levels of the Game* (New York: Farrar, Straus and Giroux, 1969), p. 45.

Chapter 4. College and Bigtime Tennis

1. Bud Collins and Zander Hollander, *Bud Collins' Modern Encyclopedia of Tennis* (Detroit: Visible Ink Press, 1994), p. 161.

2. Arthur Ashe and Frank Deford, *Arthur Ashe: Portrait in Motion* (Boston: Houghton Mifflin, 1975), p. viii.

3. Collins and Hollander, pp. 321–328.

Chapter 5. Competing for the Davis Cup

1. Arthur Ashe and Frank Deford, *Arthur Ashe: Portrait in Motion* (Boston: Houghton Mifflin, 1975), p. 121.

2. Ibid., p. 90.

3. John McPhee, *Levels of the Game* (New York: Farrar, Straus and Giroux, 1969), p. 108.

4. Ibid., p. 46.

5. Ibid., p. 118.

6. Ibid., p. 148.

7. Richard Evans, *Open Tennis, 1968–1988* (Lexington, Mass.: Stephen Greene Press, 1989), p. 44.

Chapter 6. Confronting Apartheid

1. Arthur Ashe and Frank Deford, *Arthur Ashe: Portrait in Motion* (Boston: Houghton Mifflin, 1975), p. 98.

2. Ibid., p. 107.

3. Ibid.

4. Ibid.

5. Ibid., pp. 114–115.

6. Ibid., pp. 117–118.

7. Ibid., p. 118.

8. Ibid., p. 120.

9. Bud Collins, *My Life With the Pros* (New York: E.P. Dutton, 1989), p. 222.

10. Ibid., p. 223.

11. Ibid.

12. Ibid.

13. Ashe and Deford, p. 138.

14. Ibid., pp. 140–142.

15. Ibid., pp. 144–145.

Chapter 7. A World-Class Player

1. Richard Evans, *Open Tennis, 1968–1988* (Lexington Mass.: Stephen Greene Press, 1989), p. 256.

2. Ibid., p. 134.

3. Ibid.

4. Arthur Ashe and Arnold Rampersad, *Days of Grace* (New York: Alfred A. Knopf, 1993), p. 35.

5. Frank Deford, *Arthur Ashe*, Home Box Office television documentary, September 27, 1994.

6. Ashe and Rampersad, p. 35.

Chapter 8. A Shocking End to Tennis

1. Arthur Ashe and Arnold Rampersad, *Days of Grace* (New York: Alfred A.. Knopf, 1993), p. 44.

2. Ibid., p. 70.

3. Ibid., p. 71.

4. Ibid., p. 81.

5. Ibid., p. 82.

6. Ibid., pp. 99–100.

Chapter 9. Doing Well

1. Arthur Ashe and Arnold Rampersad, *Days of Grace* (New York: Alfred A. Knopf, 1993), pp. 169–170.

2. Ibid., p. 170.

3. Ibid., p. 172.

4. Ibid.

5. Ibid., p. 173.

6. Ibid., p. 148.

7. Ibid., p. 150.

8. Ibid., p. 179.

Chapter 10. The Surgeon's Discovery

1. Arthur Ashe and Arnold Rampersad, *Days of Grace* (New York: Alfred A. Knopf, 1993), p. 202.

2. Ibid., p. 203.

3. Frank Deford, *Arthur Ashe*, Home Box Office television documentary, September 27, 1994.

4. Ashe and Rampersad, pp. 285–292.

5. Ibid., p. 290.

6. Ibid., p. 292.

7. Mary Huzinec et. al., "Man of Grace and Glory," *People Weekly*, February 22, 1993, p. 72.

8. Ashe and Rampersad, p. 127.

9. Ibid.

10. Ibid., p. 145.

11. Frank Deford, *Arthur Ashe*, Home Box Office television documentary, September 27, 1994.

Chapter 11. A Citizen of the World

1. Arthur Ashe and Arnold Rampersad, *Days of Grace* (New York: Alfred A. Knopf, 1993), acknowledgments.

2. Television broadcast of NBC-TV's *Today*, February 8, 1993.

3. Bud Collins and Zander Hollander, *Bud Collins' Modern Encyclopedia of Tennis* (Detroit: Visible Ink Press, 1994), dedication.

FURTHER READING

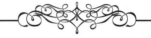

Books

Cunningham, Kevin. *Arthur Ashe: Athlete and Activist.* North Mankato, Minn.: The Child's World, 2005.

Martin, Marvin. *Arthur Ashe.* Danbury, Conn.: Franklin Watts, 1999.

McDougall, Chrös. *Arthur Ashe: Tennis Great & Civil Rights Leader.* Minneapolis, Minn.: ABDO Publishing, 2011.

Quackenbush, Robert M. *Arthur Ashe and His Match With History.* New York: Simon & Schuster, 1994.

Williams, Venus and Serena Williams. *How to Play Tennis.* New York: DK Children, 2004.

Books by Arthur Ashe

Ashe, Arthur. *Mastering Your Tennis Strokes*. New York: Macmillan, 1978.

——, et al. *A Hard Road to Glory: A History of the African-American Athlete*. New York: Warner Books, 1988.

——, and Alexander McNab. *Arthur Ashe on Tennis: Strokes, Strategy, Traditions, Players, Psychology and Wisdom*. New York: Knopf, 1995.

——, and Frank Deford. *Arthur Ashe: Portrait in Motion*. New York: Carroll & Graf, 1993.

——, and Arnold Rampersad. *Days of Grace: A Memoir*. New York: Ballantine, 1994.

——, and Neil Amdur. *Off the Court*. New York: New American Library, 1981.

INDEX